P9-AQN-153

Palazzo Falson House Museum

Fondazzjoni Patrimonju Malti
Palazzo Bonici
115, Old Theatre Street
Valletta VLT 1426
Malta
email: patrimonju@keyworld.net

© Fondazzjoni Patrimonju Malti, 2007

All rights reserved. No part of this publication may be reproduced, stored in a retrieval system or transmitted in any form or by any means without prior permission in writing by the rightful owner, nor be otherwise circulated in any form of binding or cover other than that in which it is published and without prior conditions, including this condition, being imposed on any subsequent publisher.

First published 2007

Design & Layout
Michael Lowell
Joseph Mizzi
Michelle Galea

Text
Michelle Galea
Francesca Balzan

Photography
Peter Bartolo Parnis
Jon Wrigley
Miranda Publishers
Kurt Arrigo

Produced by Midsea Books Ltd,
Carmelites Street, Sta Venera SVR1724, Malta
email: sales@midseabooks.com
for Fondazzjoni Patrimonju Malti

Printed at Gutenberg Press, Malta

ISBN: 99932-7-142-X
ISBN 13: 978-99932-7-142-0

Fondazzjoni Patrimonju Malti

Fondazzjoni Patrimonju Malti was set up as a non-profit making organisation in 1992, by a group of like-minded individuals who were intent on promoting the wealth of Maltese cultural heritage through exhibitions, research and publications. Throughout the years, *Patrimonju* has organised a number of highly prestigious exhibitions focusing on different aspects of Maltese art, which mostly featured previously unseen artefacts painstakingly sourced from private collections. The first exhibition in 1992 devoted to *Antique Maltese Clocks* turned out to be a landmark event in Malta's cultural calendar, and set the tone for the series of exhibitions to follow. A publishing division was also set up to produce the exhibitions' accompanying catalogues, but then proceeded to publish various other titles by Malta's leading academics and art historians. This division is also responsible for the highly acclaimed and avidly collected *Treasures of Malta*, a tri-annual publication containing ground breaking studies on various aspects of Maltese art, culture and history.

   Some of the other exhibitions organised by *Patrimonju* include major evaluations on Maltese silver, costume and antique furniture. Two other exhibitions, namely the one focusing on Malta's unique prehistoric art, and the maiolica exhibition, also travelled abroad, with the first being set up in Florence, and the second in Ragusa and Caltagirone, as well as The Hague.

The Palazzo Falson Project

The opening in 2007 of Palazzo Falson as an historic house museum fulfils the wish of its most recent owner and resident Capt. Olof Frederick Gollcher OBE (1889-1962). After his death, the house and its contents eventually devolved upon the *Captain O F Gollcher OBE Art and Archaeological Foundation*, which he had set up in his will with the intention that the house be opened to the public as a museum. In 2001 *Patrimonju* reached a management agreement with this Foundation, whereby it was entrusted with the conservation of the palazzo and its valuable collections, and with the setting up of a state-of-the-art museum.

   The daunting process of restoring Palazzo Falson, and its numerous unparalleled collections, commenced in 2002. The thousands of artefacts were first photographed and inventoried, and then moved to safe storage where the long task of restoring, conserving and cleaning each item was initiated. In the meantime, the building itself had to be consolidated. This meant securing the roofs, rendering the walls and ceilings waterproof, and restructuring certain areas of the building which had deteriorated beyond repair. Each stone in the building was cleaned and re-pointed using a hydraulic lime-based fill. The façade was professionally restored, as were all the wooden apertures. The wooden soffits and friezes in the three *sale nobili*, which had suffered damage from water seepage, also had to be restored. A new electrical system was installed in order to support correct museum lighting.

This arduous process of restoration was not without its rewards, as several features were discovered, shedding light on the building interventions effected throughout the centuries. Likewise, focused research on the collections revealed that certain artefacts were of exceptional importance, both on a national and international level.

dedicated to

OLOF FREDERICK GOLLCHER

1889-1962

The origins of Palazzo Falson can be traced back to the first half of the 13th century. The house was built on the remains of an even earlier structure known as *La Rocca*, which probably formed part of the defensive mechanism of Mdina in Muslim times. This area has also been associated with a synagogue, and therefore a rallying point for the Jewish community in Mdina.

Later modifications to the house carried out around the turn of the 15th century, included a change in its orientation when the present façade on Villegaignon Street was built. Architectural features of note dating to this period include a double serrated string course composed of inverted triangles terminating in ball pendants, and the hood mould above the main portal. The house was originally one storey high, and the second storey was added during the 15th century. When the house was inherited by Micheli de Falsone in 1524, further changes were made. Maltese architect Jacobo Dimeg (before 1464-before 1527) is credited with the architectural interventions that occurred in this period, and was probably responsible for the elegant two-light windows, which have become one of the most recognisable features of the palazzo.

On the arrival of the Knights of the Order of St John of Jerusalem to Malta in 1530, the house was somewhat re-modelled and improved upon in preparation for the visit of Grand Master Philippe Villiers de L'Isle Adam (r. 1530-1534). The Grand Master was accommodated in the house between the 20th October and 5th November, when he visited Mdina. It is probable that at this time the entrance hallway and the front rooms on the first floor were adapted to make them more suitable for the Grand Master's presence.

Possession of the house eventually passed from the Falsone family to the Cumbo-Navarra family and their descendants. The intervening centuries until the acquisition of the house by Olof Gollcher saw a number of changes in, and reductions of, the size of the house, some of which are still visible in the stonework of the building.

Charles Frederick de Brocktorff (1775-1850), *Palazzo Falson*, Libr. 1147 (courtesy of the National Library of Malta)

Captain Olof Frederick Gollcher was born in Valletta in 1889, the son of Chevalier Gustav Gollcher (1854-1922) and Elisa *née* Balbi (1857-1935).

Olof Gollcher was a distinguished man who received a number of honours. He joined the British Army in 1914, and served in both World Wars. He was awarded the Medal of Montenegro after the First World War, and was made a captain in 1945.

In 1936 Olof became a Knight of Grace of the Grand Priory of the British Realm of the Venerable Order of the Hospital of St John of Jerusalem, and in 1937 he was appointed Officer of the Most Excellent Order of the British Empire (OBE). In 1938 he married Teresa Lucia *née* Prior (d. 1962), known as Nella, in a London Registry Office, and then in a Catholic ceremony in Rome in 1947. Nella was an officer in the Nursing Division of St John's Ambulance Brigade, and later on became Honorary Secretary.

Olof Gollcher first purchased part of the palazzo in 1927 with his mother. The remaining portion was later acquired by him in 1938, having already inherited his mother's share in 1935. Olof set about consolidating the once fragmented property into a home, which he renamed 'The Norman House'.

Gollcher had interesting ancestors on both sides of the family. His maternal uncle was Major Henry Alexander Balbi, who translated from Spanish *The Siege of Malta 1565*. This eyewitness account was

above:
Edward Caruana Dingli (1876-1950), *Portrait of Major Henry Alexander Balbi*, 1913, oil on canvas, 111x82cm

opposite:
Giuseppe Carosi (1883-1965), *Portrait of Capt Olof Frederick Gollcher*, oil on canvas, 126x102cm

Johan Gustaf Gollcher _m_ **Maria Brigitta Wenstrom**
b. 28 Sep 1789   b. 10 Jul 1804
d. 24 Oct 1868   d. 18 May 1878

three other children

Olof Frederick Gollcher _m_
b. 2 Nov 1829
d. 15 Feb 1889

nine other children

Gustav Gollcher
b. 26 Dec 1854
d. 28 Jan 1922

Olof Frederick Gollcher
b. 17 Mar 1889
d. 23 Jul 1962

Giacomo Pantaleone Bruno ____ *m* ____ Maria Rosa Borg Olivier

_____ **Vincenza Bruno Olivier**
b. 1839
d. 27 Jul 1919

_____ *m* _____ **Elisa Balbi**
b. 23 Jul 1857
d. 16 Sep 1935

_____ *m* _____ **Teresa (Nella) Prior**
b. 1890
d. 1 Oct 1962

without issue

top:
Olof's uncle William, and aunts Rose and Sophia, his father's younger siblings (Malta, 1871)

centre:
Olof's father, grandfather and uncle James (London, August 1872)

bottom:
Olof's aunt Augusta, also known as Puscia, his father's youngest sister

11

written by Francisco Balbi da Correggio, a soldier who participated in the Great Siege under the Knights. This translation was published in Copenhagen in 1961, and included a foreword by Sir Harry Luke, who was Lieutenant Governor of Malta from 1930 to 1938, as well as Olof's friend and confidante. Major Balbi was moreover a noted researcher who published studies on the Order of St John.

Judge Giacomo Pantaleone Bruno was Olof's paternal great-grandfather, as well as a cousin of Fra Gaetano Bruno (d. 1808). Fra Bruno was the Conventual Chaplain of the Langue of Auvergne. He was also the Secretary of the Chancery of the Order of the Knights of St John during the time of Grand Masters Emmanuel de Rohan (r. 1775-1797) and Ferdinand de Hompesch (r. 1797-1798). Fra Bruno was also responsible for saving much of the Order's archives which the French intended to destroy during their occupation.

Gollcher was above all a philanthropist, as well as a passionate collector of *objets d'art* and historical relics. His forty-five collections include paintings, silver, furniture, jewellery, Oriental rugs and armoury, to mention but a few. In 1943 he proposed to donate the 'Norman House' and all its contents to the Venerable Order of the Hospital of St John of Jerusalem in the British Realm, as his wish was that the house should be open to the public as a museum. As the Order felt that it could not take on the responsibility of the house, it passed it on to the *Captain O F Gollcher OBE Art and Archaeological Foundation*, whose other aims included promoting 'more interest in the National Museum of Malta'.

Ground Floor

he courtyard is perhaps one of the best reminders of Gollcher's interest in historic revivalism. This somewhat Romantic attitude is reflected in the number of architectural and decorative elements he introduced in this area.

A very well-travelled person with a keen eye for art and architecture, Gollcher enthusiastically collected numerous pictures and photographs from palaces and various other buildings abroad, and included a number of eclectic stylistic features in his palazzo.

The Siculo-Renaissance staircase he installed in the courtyard leading to the first floor terrace, was inspired by the Sicilian examples found at Palazzo Bellomo in Syracuse, as well as at Palazzo Corvaia in Taormina.

Other notable elements in this courtyard are the fountain (detail pictured below), which was modelled after the one in the Benedictine cloister in Monreale, Sicily. This was recently restored to make it fully functional once again. Another feature Gollcher added was the Byzantine-Romanesque folly attached to a corner on the right-hand side of the courtyard. This tower-like structure is supported on columns with intricately carved capitals.

A high-relief sculpture of Grand Master L'Isle Adam's coat-of-arms was added in the 20th century to commemorate his temporary stay at the palazzo (pictured on the right).

T he refectory forms part of the oldest area of the house, and probably dates to the medieval period. The thickness of the room's walls stand testament to its antiquity.

This room was accessed from the courtyard through a pointed arch doorway, which must have been mutilated at some later stage into the present square-headed one.

A narrow arched doorway leading from the refectory into the kitchen was discovered during recent restoration works. It is one of the earliest surviving elements of the palazzo and probably belongs to the original nucleus of the house, which dates to the 13th century. This shows that the floor level in this room used to be lower than at present. The recesses and holes in the masonry around the doorway show how a wooden door would have been fitted.

On top of one of the half-cabinets in this room there is a group of clay Maltese folkloristic figurines in various poses, sharing a meal around a table, and next to this cabinet there is a small collection of spinning wheels. The larger-wheeled one is known locally as a *raddiena*, and was used to produce yarn from carded cotton. The handle-shaped crank would be turned with one hand, and would in turn set the smaller cylinders and shaft at the end of the *raddiena* spinning, while the other hand held the carded cotton which is pulled into yarn on the spinning shaft.

below:
The doorway discovered during restoration

Four Maltese formal armchairs with carved wooden front stretchers are also exhibited in this room. Their leather seats and backs are attached to the frames with brass circular studs. One of the armchairs dates to the 17th century and is decorated with cotton plant carvings on the wooden finials and stretcher. The coat-of-arms of the Cotoner Grand Masters Raphael (r. 1660-1663) and Nicolas (r. 1663-1680) can be seen at the centre of the stretcher. Armchairs such as these would feature in seated portraits of Grand Masters. The other three armchairs have acanthus leaf finials, and scroll motifs centring on a flower shape on their stretchers.

The display cabinets in this room house various small eclectic collections. One of them contains bronze petards (*maskli*), locks, various weights and measures, and pewter wares. Being a common alloy, pewter was mostly used for utilitarian items such as plates, chargers, candlesticks, tankards and flagons, and was sometimes referred to as 'poor man's silver'. This collection also includes a number of baluster-shaped measuring jugs. There is also a small collection of brass oil lamps, and candle snuffers. The window sill holds some large marble mortars.

One of the display cabinets in the refectory

The Willow pattern is one of the most famous British blue and white ceramic designs inspired by images found on Chinese pottery. It was developed in the late 18th century, and has been attributed to the potter Josiah Spode I (1733-1797). Imports from the East were much sought after at the time, and this typically Chinese design, with its pagoda, the willow tree and birds in flight, was instantly popular. Other potters also adopted it, although different makers included their own variations on the theme. The Willow pattern tells the tale of two star-crossed lovers who at the end are transformed by the gods into two immortal doves. It is thought that the fable behind these wares was enterprisingly fabricated in Britain to encourage more pottery sales.

Olof Gollcher's interest in arms and armoury is evident through the extensive and varied collection on display in this room. The walls are hung with an interesting array of swords, polearms, pistols and guns.

One of the crossbows displayed in the central showcase is a Spanish-style one that probably dates to the early 16th century. A typical crossbow is made out of a prod, similar in appearance to a bow, which is mounted on a stock. Bolts fired by crossbows were called quarrels, and were lighter than arrows. The prod and stock of early crossbows were made out of good hardwood, such as oak, but steel prods were common by the early 16th century. Along with this crossbow there is also a *pied-de-chevre*, or 'goat's foot', which is a lever designed to pull and secure the bow string behind the latch. The stock has a grooved track to guide the bolt, and the string was held in place by a nut on the bolt rest. Beneath the stock is a long iron trigger, which appeared on crossbows from the early 15th century. Crossbows were a significant military weapon in European warfare in the Middle Ages, and were abandoned during the 16th century in favour of firearms. Other items in this collection exhibited here include a heavy gauge metal Close helmet, which was one of the most common types of head protection worn by soldiers in the 16th century, as well as a selection of spurs, a brass mace, a medieval axe and a flail.

above:
Persian Dagger

left:
Persian Shield

opposite top:
Persian Helmet

The Oriental section in this armoury includes a Persian bowl-shaped spiked helmet known as a *Kulah Khud*, which is mounted with an adjustable nasal guard, two plume holders, and a chain mail neck guard suspended from the skull. This helmet is decorated with foliage and figures, and is finely damascened. This effect is achieved by inlaying soft or precious metals such as gold or silver onto a carved ground of hard metal such as iron, bronze or steel. The term 'damascening' refers to the city of Damascus, from where this technique apparently originated. This helmet probably dates to the early 19th century. The *Kulah Khud* was very popular throughout Persia and India as well as in other countries under Islamic religious and political control, and was often subject to national and regional variations. This helmet also bears an inscribed band of Kufic script along its border. Calligraphy is a fundamental

A curious item displayed in this room is a chastity belt. The chastity belt is subject to a number of myths, one of which is that it was invented in the Middle Ages to ensure fidelity while one's spouse was away crusading. However, some historians do argue that chastity belts were not medieval inventions, but products of the Victorian over-active imagination. It is said that there are no genuine chastity belts dating from the Middle Ages, and that those claimed to be such were produced in the first half of the 19th century as curiosity items. The concept of a chastity belt is said to be much older, and that reference to it in medieval poetry was used as a metaphor for pledging fidelity. This metaphorical 'belt' involved no ironwork or locks, but cloth, and was 'worn' by consensus of both parties. However, a German-written 1405 manuscript does illustrate a lockable iron chastity girdle. In recent times, many of the 'medieval' chastity belts displayed in museums were tested to confirm their age, resulting in a number of them either being removed from medieval displays, or re-dated.

21

element in Islamic art, and developed into the main form of religious ornament. Islamic arms and armour were often decorated with passages from the Qur'an, which served as talismans or expressions of piety. This section also includes a Persian round metal convex shield, known as *sipar*, and a Persian dagger. The shield has a reinforced rolled back rim, and four flower-shaped deep-domed bosses towards the centre that act as sword breakers. These bosses correspond to ring bolts at the back of the shield to which twin hand grips are attached. A fabric pad would be placed between these hand grips against which the knuckles could rest, thus allowing a firm hold. This shield is decorated with human figures in Persian-style costumes and various foliage patterns, and is damascened just like the helmet. The border is also etched with Kufic script, and with scrolling tendril motifs.

The Persian dagger, with its double-edged curved blade and "I"-shaped grip has the characteristics of the traditional *jambiya*. However, it does not contain the narrow central rib along the blade intended for reinforcement that is found in most. The term *jambiya* is the western distortion of the Arabic word *jannabiya* indicative of an item 'mounted on the hip'. Daggers were an integral part of Islamic culture, used for hunting, fighting and tribal ceremonial dances. The *jambiya* was designed for thrusting, and owing to its weight and curvature could not be thrown like other daggers. It can be found throughout the Islamic world, but is usually subject to regional variations both in style and

The stiletto dagger is a thrusting dagger with a slender tapering blade first developed in Italy. It was suitable for inflicting deep puncture wounds, or even for piercing light armour, thus making it one of the more deadly weapons. It was popular with soldiers and citizens alike due to its narrow width, and the fact that it could be both concealed and drawn with ease. The stiletto dagger was also favoured by the nobility, and was historically used by both lords and ladies. It was especially used when upper-class civilian dress incorporated mail or leather body armour. The stiletto dagger came in a variety of sizes, from small and delicate ones that could be easily hidden, to longer ones that could even be used as a *main gauche*, or parrying dagger.

top:
Turkish Yataghan

opposite bottom:
Flintlock Pistol

dimensions. The hilt and scabbard of the featured dagger are decorated with intertwined etched lines. Most *jambiyas* produced contain such carvings or acid marks, with the more elaborate ones having heavily decorated hilts, and scabbards inlaid with semi-precious stones.

The firearms section in this armoury includes a fine collection of British, Italian, French and Spanish flintlock pistols. There are also some French-style flintlock pistols that were made specifically for the Eastern markets, particularly Turkey. The flintlock was developed in France in the early 17th century, and by the second half of that century it had slowly spread throughout Europe. The simplicity of the mechanism, which incorporated the striking surface and flashpan in one piece, meant that more creative designs could be produced, such as miniature pistols. These were at times also referred to as travelling pistols.

The kitchen's architecture, as evidenced through the wall thickness, massive arches and lancet windows, dominates the room, and is a strong indicator of the medieval origins of the house.

In medieval times, when the footprint of the house was larger than it is at present, the house extended beyond the small backyard (visible from the kitchen) into the neighbouring property.

The kitchen that Gollcher affectionately referred to as his *'trattoria'*, is dominated by a large fireplace. This is decorated with colourful maiolica tiles showing individual folk figures in 18th century costume (which sometimes lean towards the Oriental). Some play musical instruments, while others engage in pastoral pursuits. There are also depictions of food and kitchen related items, and even a mouse caught in a mousetrap.

Nearby, a large wood-burning oven is similarly integrated into an architectural framework and decorated with blue and white tiles. The trapdoor in front of the fireplace leads down into a wine cellar.

A large collection of copper pots, pans, kettles, jelly moulds and containers can be seen around the room. Copper is particularly associated with the preparation of confectionery and sweets. Decorated jelly moulds resulted

Maiolica tiles from the kitchen fireplace

26

in a sweet that not only tasted good, but looked good as well. Copper kitchenware was used even before the Knights arrived in Malta, and metalsmiths are known to have been active around the Mdina area in that period.

Some furniture items of note in this room include 17th century half-cabinets known locally as *tas-sagristija* (pertaining to the sacristy), probably because such an item of furniture would be convenient for storing objects, and was often found in parish church sacristies. On top of one of these, quite close to the fireplace, are four differently-sized earthenware containers for cooking stew. These are known in Maltese as *il-baqra* (the cow). These lidded horizontally-long containers with a glazed interior stand on four squat legs, and have a head-shaped protrusion on one end. They could be placed in the oven, and were primarily used for cooking rabbit stew.

top:
Copper Lavabo

left:
Il-Baqra

bottom:
17th Century Maltese
Half-Cabinet

Not solely an admirer of the arts, Olof Gollcher also painted in oils and produced etchings and lithographs. He received his tertiary education in London, graduating as an art critic and painter.

Olof's works were exhibited at various art centres in Europe, among them the Royal Academy in London, and the *Salon des Artistes* in Paris. Hanging in this studio are a number of Gollcher's works which display a certain level of competence.

Gollcher was very fond of his pipes, which are now also displayed in his studio. He was an active member of a group of artists known as the *Confraternità della Pipa*, or the 'Brotherhood of the Pipe', and they had a seat in Via Margutta in Rome, where they held exhibitions. This brotherhood had its own emblem, costumes and rites, and held regular

Olof Gollcher with his friends and a model in his studio

parties. A 1924 parchment document of the *Confraternità* displayed here includes the signatures of some of the *compari* such as the Carosi brothers, Alberto (1891-1967) and Giuseppe (1883-1965), Enrico Ortolani (1883-c.1972) and Antonio Barrera (1889-1970). Paintings by these artists and others were donated by Gollcher to the National Museum (now the National Museum of Fine Arts).

Gollcher was also actively involved in the art scene in Malta. His diary for 1941 contains several entries noting attendance at art classes, and has him putting up an exhibition for Professional and Amateur categories at The Palace (presumably the Grand Masters' Palace in Valletta) in October and November of that year. A newspaper clipping pasted into his diary under the entry Tuesday 23rd February 1943, reports that Capt O F Gollcher OBE and others were elected to form the Committee of the Malta Art Association.

top:
Olof Collcher (courtesy of Lt. Col. & Mrs W. Attard collection)

above:
The *Confraternità della Pipa* Parchment

left:
Olof Frederick Gollcher, *Village Scene*, oil on canvas, 99x79cm

First Floor

The magnificent silver collection at the palazzo includes more than eight hundred items, consisting of some noteworthy and significant pieces of Maltese, British and Continental silver. A varied selection is displayed in the strong room, which is the location where Gollcher locked away his silver when he went away.

The flatware section of this collection includes some 18th century fiddle, thread and shell pattern table forks and spoons, engraved with coats-of-arms of Knights of the Order of St John. Several coffee pots also grace this collection, one of which is a pear-shaped one on three hoofed feet by the Maltese silversmith Michele Calleja. Tea was not generally popular in the Maltese Islands prior to the advent of the British, but coffee pot manufacturing in Malta can be traced back to the last quarter of the 17th century. Made to the Maltese standard and dating to 1838, the above-mentioned coffee pot has a raised cover with flower-spray finial, and an ebonised scroll handle.

Another elegant coffee pot is an Empire style one that stands on three paw feet legs with palmette motifs, and has an eagle head-shaped spout, and a wooden handle. The Empire style was referred to as such as it identified with the reign of Napoleon I. Evolving from the Neoclassicism of the 18th century, it was inspired by

the grandeur of ancient Egypt and Imperial Rome, and was adopted by courts across Europe, especially in Russia.

An outstanding piece in this collection is a silver nef. In old French the word 'nef' meant ship, and refers to a ceremonial object that evolved in France in the Middle Ages. Nefs were status symbols that fulfilled a number of functions, including containing salt, personal eating utensils, and napkins. They were also used for marking the place of the host or of a highly respected guest at the dinner table. In the late Middle Ages its use was widespread in France, Germany, Italy, the Low Countries and Spain. These ship models were very elaborate and precise, and included rigging, cannons and figures on deck. Eventually, some nefs stood on wheels, which meant they could be moved down the dinner table, especially useful if they were used to contain salt or even spices. In the late 16th and early 17th centuries, a great number of nefs were produced in Augsburg and Nuremberg, and in the latter city it was customary to give them as wedding gifts.

Other decorative pieces in this collection include a Maltese sugar box and cover, and numerous other sugar basins. The afore-mentioned sugar box stands on a gadrooned rim foot, and is chased with large flutes. Dating to around 1730 and bearing the assay mark only, it is also decorated with foliage and shells on a matt ground. This collection also includes a sugar basin by the Maltese silversmith Francesco Fenech. Dating to the late 18th century, it bears the eagle mark, and has a fluted pear-shaped body standing on three hoofed feet.

top left:
Silver Model of a Knight on Horseback

below:
Silver Empire Style Coffee Pot

opposite bottom:
18th Century Silver Flatware

This four-piece sterling silver oval-shaped tea and coffee service is decorated with crisp bright-cut floral sprays and cartouche engravings. The technique of bright cutting was popular in the late 18th century, and involves cutting faceted grooves into the silver, which sparkle as they catch the light. The tea and coffee pots have flush-hinged hallmarked lids, tapering spouts, and carved ivory acorn-shaped finials. The sugar bowl and cream jug have gilded interiors. Dating to 1885, this service was manufactured by the Savory brothers Joseph & Horace, and its underside is marked 'Goldsmiths Alliance Limited Cornhill, London'.

The landing on the upper floor has a sizeable collection of harbour views, ship portraits and naval engagements, as well as *objets d'art* relating to shipping.

The pair of mid-18th century landscapes hung on the facing wall as one alights from the staircase, depict the promontory of Valletta and its surrounding deep water harbours from a bird's-eye perspective. The location of the smaller harbours surrounding Valletta was ideal for the Order of St John, as galleys could shelter safely in the surrounding creeks.

The four paintings hung below depict naval engagements which resulted in spectacular captures of enemy ships and their crew by the Order's galleys. The name of the Commander of the victorious vessel is generally commemorated, as are the spoils: the quantity of cannon, people

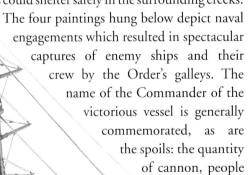

above:
G Gianni, *The 'Swalan' with Johan Gustaf Gollcher entering the Grand Harbour in 1848*, 1888, oil on canvas, 44x77cm

captured as slaves and Christian slaves liberated. The place where the encounter occurred is also recorded. These paintings have a narrative quality that show the naval action in full swing, also indicating the nearest landfall. Other paintings record important events such as the maiden voyage of the Order's squadron of ships-of-the line in 1705 (pictured on the opposite page).

An important painting displayed here is one that records an episode of Gollcher family history. It features a ship called the 'Swalan' with Johan Gustaf Gollcher as Master entering Malta in 1848. This painting depicts the vessel entering the Grand Harbour, with the Royal Naval Hospital building at Bighi in full view on the right-hand side. There were three Swedish vessels by the name of 'Swalan' that called at Malta between 1826 and 1856, two of which were under the command of Johan Gustaf Gollcher at some stage. The third vessel was also partly

Some blue and white transfer-printed Royal Navy earthenware mess plates are also displayed in this area. The mess was the area on board the ship where the crew ate together and spent much of their leisure time, and Royal Navy messes were numbered from bow to stern, odd numbers to starboard, and even to port, with each mess originally comprising a gun's crew. These plates feature the mess number and St. Edward's crown in the centre. Before 1907 naval messes had to buy their own crockery, and these plates were produced specifically for this market.

There are two main types of globes, celestial and terrestrial, which feature a map of the stars and the earth respectively, and until the late 19th century a number of these were produced as a pair. The terrestrial globe pictured on the right was made by the firm of W & T M Bardin, which was made up of William Bardin and his son Thomas Marriott. They were among the greatest globe makers in London from the late 18th through to the early 19th century. This globe has a cartouche dedicating it to the famous Sir Joseph Banks (1743-1820) a British explorer and naturalist, as well as a long-time President of the Royal Society. The cartouche also states that the globe has all the latest discoveries and communications from the most recent and authentic observations and surveys up to the year 1831. This type of globe was retailed by the scientific instrument makers and dealers W & S Jones of Holborn in London.

owned by the Gollcher family. Johan Gustaf Gollcher was the father of Olof Fredrick Gollcher, our Olof's grandfather, who founded the O.F. Gollcher & Sons Company in 1854. He was a Swede who had settled in Malta a few years earlier, and who operated ships from Malta to North Africa, Sicily and the Adriatic coast.

Four of the fifteen ship models from the palazzo's collection are displayed here, as is a selection of navigational instruments. It is said that Gollcher himself tried his hand at making similar ship models. Navigational instruments such as the octant exhibited here were designed to measure the altitude of celestial bodies above a horizontal line of reference, from which the latitude could be determined, thus giving the position at sea.

Dating to the late 18th century is a set of six harbour views hanging just above the staircase. These adopt a low view point and focus on particular areas of the harbours around Valletta. This set of prints carries the imprint *'In Firenze presso Giacomo Moro'*. They are lightly etched and heavily over-painted in gouache, and seem to follow the highly collectible sets of harbour views attributed to the mid-18th century Maltese artist Alberto Pullicino, of which few examples survive.

This coffer (or *'senduq'* in Maltese), is probably of Sicilian origin and dates to the 17th century. The history of the coffer is lost in time, but it is said to have been introduced to Malta as early as the Arab period. It was used mainly for storage, but also for sitting and sleeping on, which is why the lids of antique coffers are sometimes warped. The *senduq* characteristically formed part of the dowry given to a daughter. It would be filled with necessities such as linen etc. A small compartment inside the coffer was used to store jewellery and silver flatware.

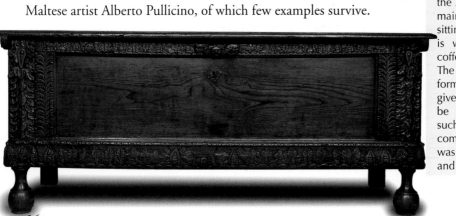

The Butler's Room

Nestling at the top of a flight of stairs from the *piano nobile* landing is a typical early 20th century bedroom for a live-in butler or servant. The 19th century lithographs hanging in the staircase record the appearance and costume of street vendors selling local produce. One of the prints depicts a Maltese lady wearing an *ghonnella* (an outer garment used by women). The *ghonnella* was an ubiquitous feature of Maltese costume, enduring for centuries until its eventual decline and complete disappearance in the second half of the 20th century.

The frame above the bed contains relics of named saints surrounded by decorative motifs. Devotional frames such as this one, crucifixes and other religious images were typically found adorning the rooms of Maltese homes (even the Tavern Scene in the painting above the dressing table shows a prominently placed image of the Virgin overseeing the gaming going on below). No bed was left unwatched by these religious paraphernalia, which were held to protect the person resting below while serving as a constant reminder to abide by the faith.

The study is mostly dedicated to Gollcher's collection of prints, which include some by well known international artists. There is also a series of naïve small-scale ancestral family portraits painted by the 19th century Swedish artist Alexis Witterbergh. The wall niche holds a number of unusual items such as opium pipes, as well as apothecary jars and some trophies.

Three of the engravings in the collection are by the German artist Albrecht Dürer (1471-1528), who is generally regarded as the greatest figure of Renaissance art in Northern Europe. Dürer expressed himself mainly through prints, as he considered paintings to be less profitable. His wife Agnes sold his woodcuts and engravings in a stall in Nuremburg's market square, as well as at fairs in other cities. The present engravings are *The Turkish Family, Three Peasants in Conversation,* and *Peasant Couple Dancing.* Dating to 1497, the first two belong to his early period, whereas the last work dates to 1514, by which time his engravings were conceived in more painterly terms.

The second set of prints in this collection are by Salvator Rosa (1615-1673), who was born near Naples, and became one of the pre-eminent 17th century Neapolitan artists. He was described by his biographers as being immensely ambitious and with a fiery temperament. These engravings belong to Rosa's best known series entitled *Figurine,* which depicts soldiers and peasant men and women. The whole series, which was executed between 1656 and 1657, was made up of sixty-two plates. His *Figurine* were very popular and were copied and imitated many times over. It is thought that Rosa produced these etchings to demonstrate his skill at depicting the human form, seeing as he was largely known for his wildly romantic and rugged landscapes including shepherds and bandits.

Another series that hangs in the study is produced after Jacques Callot's *I Balli di Sfessania.* Callot (1592-1635) was a French etcher and engraver, who studied art and print-making in Italy. *I Balli* consisted of twenty-four etchings, twenty-three of which feature paired carnival performers, and a frontispiece. Most of the figures are engaged in a high-spirited dance known in Naples as the *sfessania.* Callot's work was witty, acutely observed and skilfully rendered, and he specialised in the portrayal of beggars, caricatures, deformities and characters from picaresque novels, which were much in vogue during his time. He successfully combined the skills of a chronicler, portraitist and social historian.

top left:
Albrecht Dürer (1471-1528),
Three Peasants in Conversation,
engraving

above:
Alexis Witterbergh, *Gollcher Family Portrait,* oil on canvas, 30x23cm

bottom:
Salvator Rosa (1615-1673), from the series *Figurine,* **engraving**

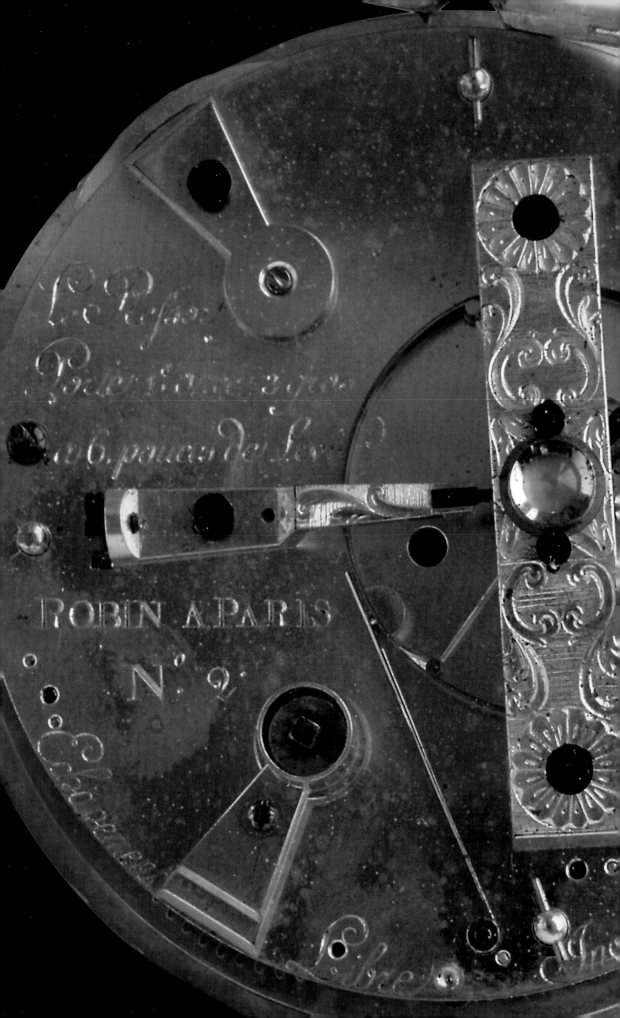

G ollcher's collection of jewellery, coins and other remarkable *objets d'art* are displayed in this room. It is also a veritable little portrait gallery of Gollcher and his contemporaries.

The two paintings of Olof and his wife Nella, facing each other on the room's upper level, were executed by the Italian artist Carlo Romagnoli (1888-1965) in 1948. Another full-length portrait of Gollcher was painted by Giuseppe Carosi, also displayed here. Both artists formed part of a group of *plein-air* painters known as '*I XXV della Campagna Romana*'.

Other portraits hung here recall some close family ties and friendships of Gollcher. The portrait of Major Henry Alexander Balbi was executed by the early 20th century leading Maltese portraitist, Edward Caruana Dingli (1896-1950). Apart from being Gollcher's uncle, Major Balbi was also his closest friend with whom he shared several interests. A portrait of another close friend, Sir Harry Luke, by the Maltese artist Toussaint Busuttil (1912-1994) also hangs in this room. Sir Harry is depicted in the robes of a member of the Venerable Order of St John of Jerusalem.

Gollcher's numismatic collection on display here includes a silver gilt medal of Grand Master Alofius de Wignacourt (r. 1601-1622) dated 1607, which is of particular importance owing to its uniqueness. Other similar medals are known in silver and bronze, but they were struck from different dies.

The jewellery items displayed in the cabinet on the left on entering the room belonged to the Gollcher family. Of particular note is the filigree necklace and matching brooch *cum* pendant with Maltese cross

The Mannerist style brooch displayed at the top of the cabinet was evidently a prized family piece and was carefully reproduced down to the smallest details in the bronze portrait bust of Olof Gollcher's mother, Elisa, which can be found in the Drawing room.

bottom left:
Silver Tetradrachm of King Ptolemy II Philadelphus (285-246 BC), obverse

bottom centre:
Sicilian Coin of Emperor Frederick II (1194-1250), reverse

bottom right:
Silver-gilt Medal of Grand Master Alof de Wignacourt, obverse

This unique watch is signed
'ROBIN A PARIS No. 2'. It
was made in Paris in 1791 by
Robert Robin (1742-1799),
King Louis XVI's favourite
clockmaker. Distinctive for
its ten-hour dial, this watch
reflects French Revolutionary
Time, which was based on
the decimal principle and was
officially adopted in 1793. It
divided the day into ten hours
with one hundred minutes each
having one hundred seconds.
Although quite simple, this
system of timekeeping did not
prove popular, and by 1795
was no longer compulsory.
On the 1st January 1806,
French timekeeping reverted
to the traditional system. Few
examples of these watches
were produced, most of which
are no longer extant.

motif, indicating their probable Maltese origin or connection. Maltese silversmiths were particularly celebrated for their fine work in filigree, several exemplars of which were displayed in the Great Exhibition of London in 1851.

The long cabinet houses a collection of small dress accessories, many of which date to the 19th century and earlier. These include *etuis*, pendants, hat pins, a silver girdle, jewellery, lockets, opera glasses, ornamental combs, a significant collection of silver snuff boxes and even a posy holder.

The collection of pocket watches includes some highly important pieces. Of particular importance is the fob watch by the Paris maker Robert Robin. Another interesting one is an open-faced quarter-repeating fob watch by the Swiss watch maker Vacheron Constantin, which dates to the early 19th century. The maker's name, serial number, type of escapement used, and

Snuff was made from a preparation of finely
pulverised tobacco that could be mixed with
lavender, cloves, jasmine, or other substances,
and then inhaled. By the 18th century, snuff-
taking was widespread throughout Europe,
and snuff boxes were frequently included
in portraits of male and female sitters. They
were produced in a variety of materials to suit
all classes and were sometimes personalized
with heraldic symbols.

the number of jewels it contains (used as bearings to reduce friction between watch movement elements), are engraved on the inner back cover. The gold encased watch signed '*S.tor Micallef & Giglio A MALTE*' probably refers to Salvatore Micallef, a securely documented 18th century Maltese clockmaker.

The small octagonal cabinet contains seals which would be hung on a fob chain attached to a waistcoat, or suspended from a chatelaine. The notable collection of rings in this cabinet includes a variety of types from rings of sentiment – such as wedding rings, and mourning rings that commemorated the passing of a loved one – to decorative rings, which include the *giardinetto* ring with jewels mounted in a flower pattern, a micro mosaic ring and rings emblazoned with Maltese crosses.

The glass collection in the long wall niche contains a varied collection. One of the earliest examples is a glass *unguentarium* dating to the Roman period. There is also a collection of Bohemian crystal decanters decorated with gold. The gold would have been applied to the glass with a sticky fixative and then fired in a kiln, thus fixing the design permanently. Of particular interest is the Bohemian crystal waterpipe reservoir decorated with gilt-painted floral swirling patterns, and enamel-painted vine leaves and grapes, which is fitted with a silver pipe attachment. Other items in this collection include the delicately painted glasses with hunting and courtly scene motifs, probably dating to the 18th century.

The collection of small silver *balsamini* (portable scent containers) includes miniature coffee pots and a particularly quaint example of a miniature bow-fronted chest of drawers. Displayed here is also a conical silver whistle decorated with *repoussé* and chased motifs. This whistle once had small attachments and a handle, transforming it into a rattle to keep young children amused.

Waterpipes such as these were inspired by Turkish *nargiles*, that originated from India or Persia, and reached the height of their popularity between the 17th and the 19th centuries. The *nargile* was an integral part of the Turkish coffee shop culture, where people sat smoking and engaged in conversation.

top:
Victorian Double-ended Scent Bottle

bottom:
Gold Filigree Hair Comb

opposite top:
Silver Filigree Necklace

The Drawing Room is one of the three main reception rooms, or *sale nobili*, in this palazzo. One of the most important paintings in this collection, located to the left of the room, is *Lucretia Stabbing Herself*, by Mattia Preti (1613-1699).

Mattia Preti (1613-1699),
Lucretia Stabbing Herself,
oil on canvas, 209x155cm

The story of Diana and Actaeon, is described at length in Ovid's Metamorphoses. While hunting in the forest, the young prince Actaeon stumbles upon Diana and her nymphs bathing by a stream. Diana, who was the virgin huntress and one of the twelve gods and goddesses of Olympus, punishes Actaeon for seeing her in the nude by turning him into a stag. This painting by an unknown artist depicts the moment that Actaeon has glimpsed Diana and is rushing away with his hands raised in astonishment, and his fate already sealed. Diana gestures in his direction while holding one of her arrows. Actaeon runs away, only to be pursued and torn apart by his own pack of dogs.

The story of Lucretia can be found in the legendary history of early Rome, as told by Livy. Lucretia was a virtuous wife of a nobleman, who was raped by Sextus, the son of the tyrant Tarquin the Proud. Sextus visited Lucretia while she was alone in her chamber, and said that if she did not give herself to him, he would kill her as well as a slave, and lay the latter's body beside her implicating her in adultery. Faced with this prospect, Lucretia yielded to him, and, after informing her husband and father, took her own life. Tarquin's nephew Brutus led a rebellion that resulted in the former's being forced into exile with his family, and in Rome's becoming a Republic.

Another interesting painting is one entitled *In the Tavern*, which has been attributed to the Flemish artist David Teniers the Younger (1610-1690). Teniers was a very prolific painter who enjoyed a good relationship with Antwerp art dealers, who appreciated the genre pieces for which he was much acclaimed. Teniers' earlier work was remarkably similar to that of Adriaen Brouwer (1605/6-1638), particularly in the use of the latter's satirical and sinister figure types, and his half-darkened interiors. Both these features are evident in the present painting.

Attributed to David Teniers the Younger (1610-1690), *In the Tavern*, oil on canvas, 30x24cm

The collection at the palazzo also includes two other paintings in Teniers' style, namely *The Monkey's Band* and *The Cat's Barbershop*, which hang in the study. Teniers was very skilled at depicting animals, and in these paintings they are humorously emulating human behaviour.

A small but remarkable portrait of a boy attributed to Bartolomé Esteban Murillo (1617-1682) also hangs in this room. Murillo lived for most of his life in his native Seville, and is mostly known for his images of gentle Madonnas, and beautiful children who are typically portrayed as poverty-stricken yet serene.

Four charming paintings attributed to Nicolas Poussin (1594-1665), featuring *putti* representing the Four Seasons, are also displayed here

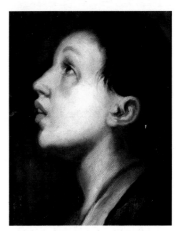

Attributed to Bartolomé Esteban Murillo (1617-1682), *Portrait of a Boy*, oil on paper, 28x22cm

(pictured above). The *putto* holding up a basket of flowers symbolises spring, the one for summer carries a sheaf of corn, while the *putto* representing autumn is depicted among vine leaves and grapes. The painting of winter features two *putti*, one of whom is crouched next to a fire, and the other *putto* is wrapped in a cloak in what is a traditional portrayal of winter. From the Renaissance onwards, *putti* feature as angels in religious works, and alongside Cupid and Venus in mythological subjects. Poussin is regarded as the founder of French Classical painting, and his style was marked by clarity and the importance given to design. During his first years in Rome, Poussin painted two bacchanals of *putti*, which specifically date to around 1626.

One of the finest pieces of furniture in the palazzo is an exquisitely decorated early 18th century Maltese chest of drawers, which stands on four bun feet separated by twin inlaid squat aprons. It is veneered with olive wood and walnut, and has four drawers, three equally deep, and a shallower top one. This chest of drawers has inlaid orange wood medallions in a lace-work design surrounded by double stringing, and is edged with ebonised mouldings. The art of inlay was introduced to the Maltese islands during the 17th century through Italian craftsmen who worked locally, many of whom would have been employed by the Knights of the Order of St. John. Chests of drawers evolved from the simple chest, or *senduq*, in the middle of the 17th century, as they were very useful in tidying away household goods.

Opposite page: The Latin word *'vanitas'* means emptiness or fickleness, and the *vanitas* theme in paintings was very popular in post-Reformation Europe, especially in Holland. Drawing inspiration from the Book of Ecclesiastes in the Old Testament, these paintings served as a reminder that all the beauty and pleasures of earthly life are transient, and that one should focus on one's mortality and the soul's redemption. Although *vanitas* paintings included lovely objects to behold, they also included references to man's mortality, such as the human skull, a burning candle, the hourglass, flowers that would soon start to fade, and rotting fruit. Musical instruments represented the pleasures of the senses, and were also the ultimate *vanitas* symbol, seeing that music ends as soon as it begins.

opposite:
Juriaen Van Streek (1632-1687), *Vanitas*, oil on canvas, 150x123cm

right:
Early 18th Century Maltese Chest of Drawers

T he Sitting Room is adorned with a number of remarkable portraits, beautiful and intricate pieces of furniture, and a selection of fine porcelain.

One of the more striking portraits in this collection is the one of a Genoese noblewoman painted after the Flemish artist Sir Anthony Van Dyck (1599-1641). Van Dyck arrived in Italy in 1621, and travelled widely therein as he wished to study the works of the great Italian masters. He made Genoa his base, where he produced a number of splendid portraits of the local aristocracy and other wealthy families. Because of his ability to capture facial features and characterise his sitters' social status, he was much sought after by Europe's nobility. Although Van Dyck was also an accomplished history painter, today he is probably better known as a portraitist. In this painting, the lady confidently

left:
After Sir Anthony Van Dyck (1599-1641), *Portrait of a Genoese Noblewoman*, oil on canvas, 70x54cm

opposite bottom:
Early 18th Century Maltese Bureau

Bas relief is sculpture executed on a flat surface, with a slight outward projection of the subjects. Aesthetically, bas relief benefits from the various depths of the incisions, and the play of light and shade on the background. The human form is particularly suited for this technique, especially in representing a group of figures in action. In Greek and Roman classical reliefs the human figure was usually portrayed in processional order, or in military and historic events. Pictured here is a detail from a stucco bas relief of the Last Supper, which is one of four displayed in this room.

looks at the viewer, reflecting the comparative independence enjoyed by Genoese women at the time, and the strong position they held both in society and within the family. She is wearing a lavish dress with a high starched ruff, and her hair is gathered beneath a cap decorated with rows of pearls and feathers.

This room also includes some magnificent pieces of furniture, such as an early 18th century bureau which has a fall-front writing surface, serpentine fronted drawers and concave sides. It is veneered with carob wood, and inlaid with double string walnut curvilinear ornamentation. Another beautiful piece is a mid-17th century Maltese side table with a long drawer and an apron, which is positioned close to the window. It is inlaid with olive wood and orange wood, and has medallions of inlaid lace-work decoration. It stands on tapering legs with ebonised mouldings, and has a cross stretcher with a mounted finial.

A number of European folding fans from a collection of more than thirty-one are also displayed in the Sitting Room. The first folding fans to be produced in Europe were inspired by examples brought over from the Orient, and by the 16th century Italy became the first European country to make them. They were soon to be produced throughout Europe, although the ones imported from China by the East India Companies remained popular. Fans had previously been a fashion accessory reserved for the aristocracy, but during the 18th century they became accessible to virtually all classes, and with the invention of lithography they became cheaper to produce and more readily available. The themes featured on these fans often reflected developments in the fine and decorative arts of the period, or were inspired by historical and cultural events. Fans were also used as means of flirtatious communication, and the way ladies held or positioned their fan would convey a message, usually to one's beloved or to would-be suitors. This code was published in contemporary magazines or etiquette books, and the British publication *The Young Ladies Journal* of 1872 reported on the significance of these gestures.

The typical Maltese wall clock (pictured on the opposite page) had a painted and gilt case, and apart from telling the time also served a decorative purpose. Its origins date to the 17th century, and it is thought that it was created indigenously. Its framework has been compared to the box-like street niches containing religious statues, from where a more decorative and elaborate case could have developed. These clocks were usually found in prominent places of upper-class houses, palaces and

Table-cabinets were created for the storage of papers, jewels, and other valuables. Designed to stand on tables or other chests, they came into fashion in the 16th century, although later on cabinets with their own legs were also produced. Cabinets were important pieces of furniture, especially because of the value of their contents, and, as precious woods were used, the best craftsmanship was lavished on their production. Consequentially, the cabinet-maker became a very highly regarded craftsman. The cabinet was ultimately to grow in size, and was often the dominant piece of furniture in the room. The drawers of this table-cabinet include glass painted panels with mythological scenes, and is one of nine found around the palazzo.

left:
Maltese Wall Clock

bottom:
Capodimonte Porcelain Figure of
Venus

opposite top:
Brisé Fan

convents, especially during the late 18th century. They could also be found in the Grand Master's Palace and the Auberges, and it is said that some servants were specifically employed to dust, wind and adjust these timepieces. The dial, which was left white, was made out of wood and had layers of gypsum applied to it. It was then decorated with floral motifs, birds, landscapes and other scenery. These clocks continued to be produced well into the 19th century.

The wall niche in this room holds some Capodimonte figurines. The origin of Capodimonte porcelain dates back to 1743 when Charles VII, King of the Two Sicilies, instigated experiments of porcelain production in the grounds of the Royal Palace at Capodimonte outside Naples. A formula for distinctive soft-paste porcelain was developed, and its pronounced creamy colour and clear glaze made it particularly ideal for undecorated porcelain sculpture. When Charles assumed the Spanish throne in 1759, he moved his factory to the Buen Retiro Palace outside Madrid, to preserve the secret of its manufacture. His son Ferdinand succeeded him to the Neapolitan throne, and eventually ordered the founding of a new factory in Portici, where production began in 1772. The style and decoration closely resembled that of the original Capodimonte factory. The production of this fine luminous porcelain reached its peak in the late 18th century when it became famous throughout Europe.

T

he Dining Room is dominated by a magnificent fireplace, the hood of which bears Grand Master L'Isle Adam's coat-of-arms, and an inscription commemorating his visit to the palazzo.

This room also has a painted frieze of garlands of fruits and flowers, which was executed by the Maltese artist Victor Fleri Soler (1898-1959), in some instances with the help of Olof Gollcher himself. Fleri Soler was known for his small scale interiors and still life paintings, and for polychromatic flowers against delicate backgrounds. The numerous paintings in this room include portraits of Olof's parents and grandparents, various landscapes and still life compositions. At one end of the room, there is a classically-inspired marble portrait bust of Napoleon Bonaparte, that was modelled after the official one made by Antoine-Denis Chaudet (1763-1810) in 1804. A plaster mould was sent to Carrara, where, starting in 1807, 1,200 replicas were produced.

The Dining Room table is laid out with a fine array of silverware, including cutlery from a canteen of Victorian Queen's Pattern flatware. These were manufactured by the afore-mentioned Savory Brothers. A Dutch silver nef that probably dates to the second half of the 19th century is situated at one end of the table. Also gracing this table are a selection of fine Venetian armorial glasses. These bear the coat-of-arms of Fra Gaetano Bruno.

One of the finest pieces in the palazzo's silver collection is the covered jug by Gioacchino Lebrun that belongs to the time of Grand Master De

Still life painting features inanimate objects including flowers, tables set with food, or, as in the featured painting, the results of a successful hunt. These hunting trophy paintings were favoured because of their decorative qualities, as well as for their association with a privileged lifestyle, owing to the fact that hunting was a sport reserved for the nobility. Although the development of the still life genre occurred mainly in the Netherlands, this tradition took hold as well in Italy and Spain. Gollcher frequently went on shooting trips abroad, and these paintings may have been to his taste.

Rohan. It is made to the Roman standard of 11 deniers, and bears the mascle and eagle marks. The jug *per se* (excluding the feet) is inspired by the designs of French silversmiths in the Louis XVI period. It could have been made after a model by the French silversmith Robert-Joseph Auguste (1723-1805), who made numerous items for the French court, and whose other prominent patrons included George III and Catherine the Great. This jug has an elongated pear-shaped body, on bifurcated scroll feet applied with shells and acorn leaves. The handle is fashioned out of intertwined vine tendrils, thus indicating that it might have been used as a claret jug.

One of the landscapes displayed in the dining room is by Richard Parkes Bonington (1802-1828). Bonington was the son of a provincial drawing-master

The Schranz family of artists are particularly associated with topographic and harbour views. Originally hailing from Germany, the artist Anton Schranz (1769-1839) married in Minorca and later settled in Malta, where he and his sons firmly established themselves as topographic artists. The signature 'A. Schranz' was discovered during recent conservation treatment of the featured painting, and may tentatively be associated with either Anton Schranz or, perhaps more plausibly, with his son Antonio (1801-?), who was also a skilled painter of views in a somewhat Romantic vein. Antonio travelled widely in the Eastern Mediterranean. The landscape featured in this painting, with its verdant hills, river, and hilltop town with gabled roofs depicts a foreign land.

left:
Late 18th Century Silver Covered Jug

opposite right:
Dutch Silver Nef

opposite bottom:
Giuseppe Recco (1634-1695), *Still Life with Dead Game*, oil on canvas, 77x104cm

and painter, and was an accomplished watercolourist from an early age. He was known for his landscapes, which he exhibited at the Paris Salon of 1822 and 1824. In the latter he won a gold medal for his originality and atmospheric effects. Each summer Bonington would set off on a sketching tour, visiting places like Normandy, Picardy and Flanders, and in 1826 he travelled to Venice, where he produced some of his finest works. Unfortunately Bonington died of consumption at the age of 26.

Richard Parkes Bonington (1802-1828), *Coastal Scene with Fishing Boats* (detail), oil on canvas, 40x60cm

Olof Gollcher seems to have been quite fond of the ornamental nature of Hanau silver, as a number of such pieces are found in the palazzo's collection. Hanau was an important manufacturing centre for highly decorative and ornate pieces, and its silversmiths were very skilled. This collection includes these silver models of a Knight and Queen that bear the marks associating them with the Neresheimer firm. This firm was founded in 1890 by August and Ludwig Neresheimer with Jean Schlingloff. They produced a number of decorative objects, such as tankards, nautilus cups and nefs, and even figures and animals, a number of which were made specifically for the British market.

Olof Gollcher's collection of over 4,500 books is housed in this library. For a private collection it is considerably large and must have been put together over decades of collecting.

A photograph taken in the early 1930s shows a row of two-metre high mahogany cupboards containing around two hundred books. This collection gradually expanded in size as well as subject matter, necessitating more wooden shelving and a walkway, which were set up above the existing cupboards. The library walls now had floor-to-ceiling shelving, as can be seen in the above photograph.

The subjects covered by this collection are numerous, ranging from the art of ancient warfare to the two World Wars, from medieval history to mineralogy, or from the Court of the French Kings to curiosities such as books about poisoners. There are several biographies on prominent persons and artists, and a particularly extensive collection of British history books. The vast selection of art historical books and periodicals reflect Gollcher's collecting interests.

above:
The library during Olof
Gollcher's lifetime

opposite top:
One of the manuscripts
in the library

Some prestigious multi-volume sets include the 9th edition of the *Encyclopaedia Britannica*, published between 1875 and 1889 in 25 hefty leather-bound volumes. A more voluminous set is the one featuring the complete works of Voltaire, which were published from 1785 to 1789 in 70 volumes. Other sets of interest include Pastor's *The History of the Popes (1305-1700)*, edited by F.I. Antrobus and published in 1923,

The portrait of a man displayed in the library is by Charles Beale, who hailed from a family of painters. Both his maternal grandfather and his father were amateur painters, and his mother, Mary Beale (1633-1699), was the most prominent and prolific female portrait painter in England in the 17th century. Her close circle of friends was made up of a number of illustrious personages, including Sir Peter Lely, who was the court painter of King Charles II. Lely's stylistic influence is evident in Mary's work, and it is believed that he passed on portrait commissions he did not want to carry out himself. She was also one of his most sought after copyists. Charles Beale was, along with his brother Bartholomew, an assistant in his mother's studio, where they painted cartouches and finished off the drapery in her portraits. Charles went on to have a successful career of his own, and is even known for his portrait miniatures. He also produced a number of remarkable red-chalk studies of family members and friends, which are among some of his most accomplished works.

and the *Cambridge Modern History*, published in 14 volumes between 1904 and 1912.

Gollcher's library also includes numerous Melitensia books (pertaining to the Maltese Islands or by Maltese authors), all of which have become highly collectible. Prominent among them are the two official histories of the Order of St John, namely, *Dell'Istoria della Sacra Religione*, by Giacomo Bosio, and continued by Bartolomeo Del Pozzo, and the Abbe de Vertot's *Histoire des Chevaliers Hospitaliers de S. Jean de Jerusalem* (1726). A version of the latter in English, entitled *The History of the Knights of Malta* (1728) is also present in this collection.

A number of Old Paris porcelain apothecary jars can also be found in the library. They were used to store medicinal drugs, herbs and spices, as well as perfumes and cosmetics. The name of the *materia medica* is written on each jar in abbreviations, at times also indicating what form the particular medicinal was under. Some abbreviations used were *'Pil'* for pills, *'Ung'* for ointment, *'Pulv'* for powder, and *'Tr'* for tincture. They are decorated with multi-coloured flowers, foliage, and gold-painted bands. They also feature the serpent, which amongst its various meanings symbolises wisdom, immortality and healing. The serpent coiled around the bowl of Hygeia, the Greek goddess of health, is a widely known pharmaceutical symbol.

above:
Dell'Istoria della Sacra Religione et Ill.ma Militia di San Giovanni Gierosolimitano, Parte Seconda by Giacomo Bosio. This edition was published in Rome in 1594.

below:
Old Paris Porcelain Apothecary Jar

A number of icons adorn the walls of the chapel, including two of the Virgin and Child which are encased within *rizas*, denoting them as objects of special veneration.

The word 'icon' is derived from the Greek word *eikon*, meaning image, and icons are generally associated with Eastern Orthodox Christianity. They illustrate stories from the Bible, and the lives of the Saints. Icon painters prepared themselves for their work by fasting and praying. *Rizas* are decorative metal covers, usually silver, that only reveal the painted faces and areas of bare flesh, and were used for enhancement and protection from human handling. One of the two Virgin and

left:
18th Century Greek School, *Icon of the Virgin Holding a Crucifix*, oil on panel, 36x26cm

opposite top:
18th Century Sicilian School, *St Angelo Martyr*, oil on canvas, 183x136cm

opposite bottom:
Icon of the Virgin Eleousa (detail), tempera on panel covered with silver riza, 46x36cm

Child icons is of the traditional *Eleousa* type, also known as the Virgin of Tenderness or Mercy. The iconography of the *Eleousa* usually depicts the faces of the Virgin and Child touching affectionately, and the Child with an arm wrapped around the Virgin's neck.

A third icon in this chapel is a Greek 18th century one featuring a sorrowful Virgin holding the crucifix in her arms. The maphorion, or veil, worn by the Virgin is of a deep red colour, symbolising her love for her Son, while at the same time referring to the blood that Christ has shed for mankind's salvation. It also has three gold star-crosses, which symbolise the Holy Trinity. She is set against the traditional gold background, which represents the Divine Light.

In another icon St Nicholas is depicted blessing with one hand, while holding a Gospel Book in the other. He is flanked by images of Christ and the Virgin on a bank of clouds, handing him a Gospel book and the omophorion (Episcopal stole) respectively. St. Nicholas was bishop of Myra in Asia Minor in the 4th century, and is the patron saint of children, sailors, travellers, and the guardian of nubile maidens. He eventually also became the inspiration for Father Christmas.

The painting over the altar in the chapel is of St Angelo Martyr, and is probably the work of an 18th century Sicilian artist. Flanking the altar

are two silver processional lanterns with the Cross of the Order that also date to the 18th century. On the jambs of the arch, there are two small silver holy water fonts intended for domestic use. Some of these private fonts were often quite ornate, in materials such as gold or silver, and adorned with enamel and pearls. Eventually their shape developed

Metal icons were popular in the 18th and 19th centuries, and are largely associated with the Old Believers, a conservative sect of Russian Orthodox Christians. These icons were portable and durable, with the ones portraying patron saints usually given to travellers and soldiers for protection, and were often worn on a string around the neck despite being relatively heavy. Small metal icons and crosses had been introduced from Byzantium during the 10th century, and came into production following Russia's conversion to Christianity. At the centre of the Nativity composition is the recumbent figure of the Virgin Mary, with the star at the top that leads the magi to the birthplace of Jesus. He is depicted in swaddling clothes in a manger within a cave, reminding us of the tomb He was later buried in. Joseph is portrayed at the bottom left-hand corner next to midwives attending to bathe the Child, a detail that is derived from the apocryphal Gospel of Matthew. The bath is styled as a baptismal font that symbolises the immaculate womb of the Virgin, and rebirth through purification.

left:
Silver Holy Oil Flasks

bottom left:
Silver Holy Water Stoup

below:
18th Century Maltese Silver Reliquary

opposite:
A Maltese Wedding, oil on canvas, 67x86cm

into a round basin attached to the wall by means of a plate. The shell-shaped basin, which appears on fonts in general, was introduced in the 17th century. The present fonts are executed with great detail, and feature a pair of birds drinking at a fountain, as well as baskets of flowers, ribbons, fruit and foliage. They are the work of the silversmith Bartolomeo Valazza, who operated in Venice in the first half of the 19th century.

The intricately carved cabinet in the Chapel holds a number of silver ecclesiastical pieces, such as three 17th century holy oil flasks. These narrow-necked pear-shaped flasks have screw-on cylindrical lids with baluster finials. Decorated with scrolling foliage and rosettes, their respective bodies are also inscribed with the letters *'CAT'*, *'CHR'* and *'INF'*, which stand for *Catechumeni*, *Chrisma* and *Infirmorum*. There is also a portable holy water stoup that possibly dates to the late 17th century. Its bulbous body has a lobed rim, and is chased with large flutes at the base. The swing handle, whose attachments are decorated with cherub heads, has a ball finial and pendant ring. The holy water stoup is usually accompanied by a sprinkler also known as an aspergillum, which comes from the Latin word *aspergere*, meaning to sprinkle.

71

D ominated by the four poster bed, the bedroom also contains some noteworthy female portraits which date to the 18th century.

left:
Female Saint, oil on panel, 34x26cm

below:
Anonymous 18th Century, *Portrait of a Girl Holding a Flower and a Fan* (detail), oil on canvas, 118x91cm

opposite:
Anonymous 18th Century, *Portrait of a Maltese Lady*, oil on canvas, 104x76cm

To the left of the bed is a full length portrait of a girl. Painted in a rather naïve style, the artist carefully depicts her elegant stomacher and shoes, the closed fan in her hand, and the jewellery she wears. Hanging above the cabinet is an 18th century seated anonymous portrait of an elderly lady, which is remarkable for the depiction of the costume of Maltese ladies of the period. The starched white wimples and lace ruffs introduce the only relieving element in the otherwise dark costume, which borders on the austere. Next to this painting is a portrait of a young girl. This portrait is most unusual in that the sitter wears plain, unadorned clothes. She holds a book aloft and points towards it. It has been suggested that this may refer to a bible and that the portrait hints at the girl's intended future in religious life.

A pair of early 20th century silk embroidered panels also hangs in this room. They are of Far Eastern origin, possibly Chinese, and are embroidered with silk and gold metal threads on purple silk satin. They feature the peacock, which is a symbol of beauty and dignity. Embroidery is an important and sophisticated Oriental art form, and Chinese embroidery was one of the main products transported along the ancient Silk Road. China was the first country in the world that discovered the use of silk, and the production of silk threads and fabrics led to the art of embroidery, which became widespread during the Han Dynasty (206 BC-220 AD).

The beautifully carved cabinet in the master bedroom contains a number of purses and handbags, and other clothing accessories. There

above:
Maltese Lace Fan

left:
The display cabinet in the master bedroom

76

are also some of Olof Gollcher's personal effects, like membership cards of the various clubs and organisations he belonged to, as well as some of the medals he received. At the centre of the cabinet there is a Maltese lace fan that probably dates to the late 19th century. It is mounted on silver sticks and guardsticks, and the latter are elegantly engraved with a floral motif. The fine beige silk lace is of a typical design of the 19th century *Maltese Blonde*. Another fan in this cabinet is a 19th century Cantonese one, which is also known as a Mandarin fan or 'thousand faces' fan. The sticks and guards are made out of lacquered wood, and the leaf is made out of paper painted with gouache and ink. The Mandarin fan typically featured court or pavilion scenes with numerous figures, with the reverse side often featuring Chinese port scenes, birds, flowers, or children at play. The process of making these fans was quite laborious, as one of the tasks included individually applying ivory faces and silk gowns to the many figures on the leaf. Mandarin fans were designed solely for export to Western markets, and were particularly popular in the second and third quarters of the 19th century. Their popularity made them the subject of many myths, one of which claimed that the faces of the figures were made out of human fingernails instead of ivory. This cabinet also contains a lockstitch sewing machine produced by William Taylor of Driffield, England, in the 1870s.

The French term *Prie Dieu* refers to a kneeler or prayer desk. These were first used in the Middle Ages during religious services by the higher clergy, but were eventually used both in churches and in domestic homes. This Maltese walnut mid-17th century *prie dieu* incorporates a cupboard where prayer books could be kept, as well as a storage space for a kneeling cushion, and is decoratively inlaid with orange wood and olive wood. In affluent homes, a *prie dieu* was often placed beside the bed, beneath a religious picture.

Palazzo Falson has an impressive collection of over eighty Oriental rugs from different areas such as Azerbaijan, Afghanistan and Turkmenistan. This collection also includes some Persian and prayer rugs.

Historical sources claim that Azerbaijan was one of the most important carpet-weaving centres in the East in the Middle Ages. Rugs were made to satisfy both utilitarian and aesthetic needs, and in Azerbaijan the rugs were woven by women, with methods that were passed on from one generation to the next. Rugs would also form part of a girl's dowry, which she had to help weave.

Animals, vegetation and irrigated fields were elements from everyday life that inspired the Turkmen carpet weavers. The general designs are of an emphatic national character, and have been preserved for centuries as they were passed on from one generation to the next. This collection includes two Turkmen *chuval* bag faces. A *chuval* is a large carpet-like bag for the storage of clothes and household things. Just the front panel of the *chuval* is usually seen in the west, as the bag face was easier to display, and in the past many carpet dealers removed the backs. The highly stylised

above:
Azerbaijan Rug, 186x132cm

opposite:
Azerbaijan Rug, 170x120cm

floral motif repeated in the main field is known as a *gul*, which is the Persian word for flower. *Guls* are the primary elements in these rugs, and may differ from one Turkmen carpet to the next, as each tribe had its own unique variation. The *chuvals* in this collection have the characteristics of the Yomud tribe, who were prolific weavers famous for their *asmalyks*, which are camel-flank hangings.

Prayer rugs are used by Muslims to kneel on while they pray, and are immediately folded and put away until their next use to ensure that they remain clean. They have a directional design characterised by the prayer niche, or *mihrab*, at one end of the carpet which must point towards Mecca when one is praying. One of the prayer rugs in this collection is an Afghan Baluch one. The nomadic Baluch tribe can be found in the areas of Khorassan, Afghanistan and Turkmenistan, and their rugs are usually adorned with geometric and stylised motifs of leaves and flowers. The niche on the featured rug is formed out of a rectangular gable, which is flanked by two rectangles containing stylised plant-shaped motifs where the hands are positioned. The colours used by the Baluch tribe were predominantly dark blue, earthy reds, burgundy, dark brown and touches of ivory. These rugs were made entirely out of

Turkmen Chuval, 125x77cm

Edward Lear (1812-1888) was an English artist, author and traveller, who today is probably better known for his Nonsense verses, and the whimsical poem 'The Owl and the Pussycat'. Throughout his life, Lear travelled extensively throughout Europe, the Middle East and India, visiting places that at the time were off the beaten track, and often despite difficult weather conditions. He never missed an opportunity to sketch and to record his impressions of that particular place in his journals, or in his letters home. Lear first came to Malta in 1848, again in 1849, and also spent the winter months of 1865 to 1866 on the island. This watercolour was a gift to Olof Gollcher from Sir Harry Luke.

wool, but the ends and edges were often reinforced with goat hair. Each Baluch rug is one of a kind, as no duplicates were produced.

The Afshars are an ancient nomadic Turkic tribe that moved from Central Asia into Iran around 1000 years ago, where they dispersed throughout the country. The Afshar tribeswomen weave the rugs on horizontal looms, combining handspun wool with cotton to produce rugs that are usually square. Identifying an Afshar rug can be difficult due to the variety of patterns adopted, as the tribe would have picked up diverse influences on their travels. However, a strong indication is given through the weaving method of combining semi-depressed warps with symmetrical knotting and double wefting, which was their most common technique. The Afshar rug in this collection has all the qualities of the traditional type produced in the city of Sirjan, in the Kerman province. The characteristically geometric patterns feature a line of diamond-shaped medallions in the centre of the rug, surrounded by other small animal or plant motifs, within borders of stylised rosettes and vines. The colours used are predominantly red, burgundy, navy blue and ivory.

Capt Gollcher was a member of the Antiquities Committee, and actively spoke in favour of the preservation of Maltese historical sites. He was also the secretary of both the *International Institute of Mediterranean Archaeology* and its local offshoot, *The Malta Underwater Archaeological Branch*, which was set up in 1961.

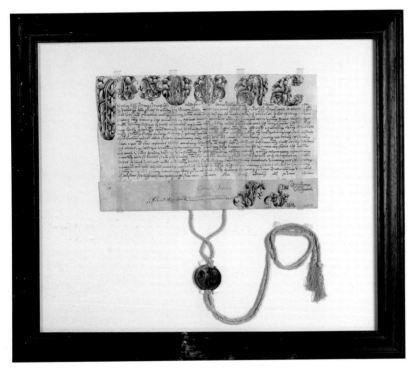

Gollcher actively endeavoured to raise awareness of the institute's activities in the press. The headquarters of the local branch was located at this palazzo, where a laboratory for the cleaning of pottery and metals was also set up. Gollcher himself had actually followed a course in Italy to learn about cleaning and consolidating finds made on land and under the sea. The institute's team was successful in recovering objects of historical value around Malta and Sicily, most of which were presented to local museums. The Archaeological Collection displayed at the palazzo contains some Roman pieces, including an early trefoil-lipped jug with a flat base, a dipping cup and an *unguentarium*. There is also a variety of oil lamps, bowls and parts of amphorae. Other interesting pieces include an ancient clay figurine of a female figure with head-dress, and an archaic type marble bearded head, possibly of a divinity.

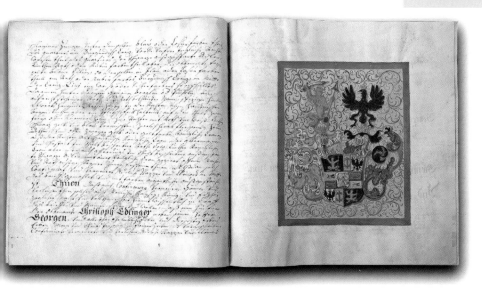

The documents on display in this room include seven papal bulls, one of which is pictured on the opposite page. A papal bull is an official written communication issued under the authority of the pope by the Vatican Chancery. The term 'bull', or *bulla* in Latin, refers to the seals with which these documents were authenticated, and eventually was used to refer to the document itself. The seals were mostly made out of lead (with gold being used in special circumstances), and depicted the heads of St. Peter and St. Paul on the obverse, and the name of the issuing pope on the reverse. The seal was attached to the document by a cord made out of hemp, or yellow and red silk. The first line of the bull was written in tall elongated letters that featured the pope's name, and his title *Episcopus Servus Servorum Dei* (Bishop, Servant of Servants of God). These were followed by the opening words of the text, called the *incipit*, from which the title was derived.

One of the documents in this room is an illuminated manuscript, and on one of its pages is a miniature featuring a full armorial bearing of a nobleman (pictured above). The shield is surmounted by two crowned helmets each carrying a separate crest and full mantling. The colours used in this miniature have been well preserved. A gold frame surrounds the miniature, and further gold highlights embellish the coloured passages. The document itself appears to be written in German and has decorated initials on the front page. It contains signatures on the back, and traces of a red wax seal.

A Selection of Artefacts from the Archaeological Collection

Abela, A E, *Governors of Malta*, Progress Press, Malta 1991.

Antique Marks, Collins, London 2006.

Apap Bologna, Alaine, *The Silver of* Malta, MAG Publications, Malta 1995.

Attard, Robert, 'Arms and Armour at Palazzo Falson', *Treasures of Malta* Vol.VII No.2, Easter 2001, pp. 67-71.

Azzopardi, Consiglia, *Il-Bizzilla tal-Gzejjer Maltin*, Publikazzjonijiet Indipendenza, Malta 2003.

Azzopardi, Emmanuel, 'Numismatic Collection at Palazzo Falson', *Treasures of Malta* Vol.XI No.3, Summer 2005, pp. 37-43.

Buhagiar, Mario, *The Late Medieval Art and Architecture of the Maltese Islands*, Fondazzjoni Patrimonju Malti, Malta 2005.

Buhagiar, Mario, 'The Palazzo Falsone at Mdina - An Art Historical Appreciation', *Treasures of Malta*, Vol.XII No.2, Easter 2006, pp. 15-18.

Buhagiar, Mario and Fiorini, Stanley, *Mdina - The Cathedral City of Malta* (2 Vols.), The Central Bank of Malta, Malta 1996.

Burstyn, Dorothea, 'The Antique Silver Industry in Hanau', *Silver Magazine*, Sep-Oct 1997.

Cauchi, John A, *Catalogue of Paintings Watercolours Prints and Reliefs in the Palazzo Falzon known as "The Norman House" Mdina*, Malta 1973.

Cutajar, Dominic, 'The Gifted Schranz Family: Anton and Giovanni', *Treasures of Malta*, Vol.IV No.3, Summer 1998, pp. 7-11.

Farrugia, Jimmy, *Antique Maltese Domestic Silver*, Said International, Malta 1992.

Farrugia, Jimmy, *Antique Maltese Ecclesiastical Silver*, Progress Press, Malta 2001.

Galea-Naudi, Joseph and Micallef, Denise, 'Coffers and Candle Boxes', *Treasures of Malta*, Vol.I No.2, Easter 1995, pp.58-61.

Gambin, K and Buttigieg, N, *Storja tal-Kultura ta' l-Ikel f'Malta*, Pubblikazzjonijiet Indipendenza, Malta 2003.

Gatt, Ġużi, *Qiegħda fil-Ponta ta' Lsieni*, Klabb Kotba Maltin, Malta 2005.

Hall's Dictionary of Subjects and Symbols in Art, John Murray Limited, London 1996.

Holmes, Richard (Ed.), *Weapon - A Visual History of Arms and Armour*, Dorling Kindersley Limited, London 2006.

Manduca, John (Ed.), *Antique Furniture in Malta*, Fondazzjoni Patrimonju Malti, Malta 2002.

Manduca, John (Ed.), *Antique Maltese Clocks*, Progress Press Co. Ltd., Malta 1992.

Micallef, Mark (Ed.), *Silver and Banqueting in Malta*, Progress Press Co. Ltd., Malta 1995.

Miller's Antiques Encyclopedia, Mitchell Beazley, London 1998.

O'Brien, Bill, 'Naval Mess Plates and Bowls', *Treasures of Malta*, Vol.X No.2, Easter 2004, pp. 65-67

Osborne, Harold (Ed.), *The Oxford Companion to Art*, Oxford University Press, Oxford 1970.

Sammut, Joseph C, 'Unique Gilt Silver Wignacourt Medal Discovered at Palazzo Falson', *The Sunday Times* (Malta), 5 December 2004.

Truman, Charles (Ed.), *Sotheby's Concise Encyclopedia of Silver*, Conrad Octupus Limited, London 1996.

Wettinger, Godfrey, 'The Falzon Family and the Capomastro of its House at Mdina', *Storja 2003-2004*, Malta University Historical Society, Malta 2004, pp. 21-33.

apron	a shaped piece of wood that runs beneath a chest of drawers
armorial	featuring a crest or coat-of-arms
bacchanals	a term pertaining to Bacchus, the god of wine, and used to refer to a drunken celebration
balsamina	the term is derived from the word 'balsam', and is locally used to refer to a vinaigrette, which was a little box containing a small sponge soaked in aromatic vinegar or perfume
bosses	an ornamental knoblike projection
capitals	the top, or crowning feature of a column
cartouche	an ornamental frame in the form of a scroll
Catechumeni	refers to the holy oil used in the sacrament of Baptism
chasing	method of decorating silver (or other metals), by using punches or hammers to achieve a relief effect
chatelaine	a chain worn at the waist by women, from which a number of items such as keys, a pair of scissors, a watch and a purse were suspended
Chrisma	refers to the holy oil used during the sacrament of Confirmation
deniers	unit measuring the fineness of silver indicating to which standard it belonged (eg: during the Knights' period, the French standard was of 11.5 deniers, the Roman standard was of 11 deniers and the Maltese standard was of 10.5 deniers)
ebonised	wood stained in black to emulate ebony
escapement	a mechanism used in timepieces that regulates the movement of the wheel
etching	an impression taken from an etched plate, the design of which was created through the corrosive action of acid
etui	a term derived from French, and used to refer to a little decorative case within which small objects such as needles, scissors and tweezers were kept
fiddle, thread and shell pattern	flatware featuring a fiddle-shaped handle, single or double lines of incised threading, and a shell motif at the handle terminal
finial	a decorative termination on top of a piece of furniture

folly — a whimsical structure, usually built to serve as a conversation piece

gadrooning — decorative edging that consists of vertical, convex or spiralling curves

hood mould — a projecting moulding above a doorway, window or arch

illuminated manuscript — refers to books written by hand and decorated with various paintings

Infirmorum — refers to the holy oil applied on a sick person during Extreme Unction

lancet window — slit-like window

lithograph — an impression printed from a specially prepared stone slab

materia medica — substances used for preparing medicine

naïve — refers to a painting executed in a simple unaffected style

plein-air — pertaining to painting executed outdoors, characterised by natural luminosity and atmosphere

putto — a representation of a cherubic infant

repoussé — the process of chasing embossed metal to refine its design

sterling silver — silver items having a standard fineness of 92.5 per cent purity

stretcher — a rail that joins and stabilises the legs of a chair or a table

string course — a continuous horizontal decorative band

unguentarium — a container used to store oils or perfume

warp — the foundation material of a carpet that is generally made of cotton, wool or silk

waterpipe — a smoking device with a long flexible tube that passes through a water reservoir, which cools the smoke as it is drawn through

weft — horizontal threads interwoven with the warps of a rug

yataghan — a type of Turkish sword used from the 16th to the 19th centuries